Ashes of a Valleys Childhood

Ashes of a Valleys Childhood

by Lynda Nash

with a foreword by
Barrie Llewelyn

MULFRAN PRESS

Published 2009 by Mulfran Press
PO Box 812, Cardiff CF11 1PD
UK
www.mulfran.co.uk

The right of Lynda Nash
to be identified as author of this work has been
asserted in accordance with the Copyright,
Designs and Patents Act, 1988.

ISBN 978-1-907327-01-8

Printed by imprint**digital** in Devon.
info@imprintdigital.net

Acknowledgements:

I'd like to say thank you to tutor June Lane who inspired me to write by reading Gillian Clarke's *Miracle On St David's Day*, to Penyrheol Spiritualist Church Open Circle for encouraging me to read poetry aloud, to my nephew Dan Curtis who was there when *Ashes of a Valleys Childhood* was just a title, and to my editor, Leona Carpenter, and Barrie Llewelyn for their feedback. And of course to Dave, Ryan and Ceri who put up with having a writer in the family.

Some of the poems in this collection, or earlier versions of them, first appeared in the following publications: *Daps, Eclipse, Purple Patch, The Ugly Tree*.

In loving memory of Ifor Miles Watkins

Contents

Foreword

Lynda Nash would tell you that she is not a poet. This is an odd way to begin an introduction to Lynda's first collection of poetry, *Ashes of a Valleys Childhood*, but it's true. She would say that she is a prose writer who sometimes turns memories into something that resembles a poem. I don't agree with her. We've had this discussion for a few years while these poems have come out of dusty ring binders and been found in old computer files; while new ones have been born. While they have been revised, reworked, ordered, and finally, made into a collection. All the time Lynda has been protesting and I have been arguing with her.

So why are they poems? Look at the subject – a particular childhood in a particular place – and the unsentimental way in which it's examined and you will find the poet's soul. These are honest portraits of eccentric family members and puzzling situations – often looked at from the child's eye and yet told with sophistication that can only come from looking back upon a thing. Memory can distort but it can also add clarity. In choosing the exact right word to put in the exact right place, the mixture of innocent questioning and the maturity of acceptance are conveyed. Yet the acceptance never means that a peculiar situation, an adult's unexpected and unexplained reaction, is not thought about and does not continue to be examined. There is an on-going wonderment in these poems; the kind of wondering that may never reach a conclusion.

The exact right word in the exact right place. Look at 'A Day Off', the ordinariness of:

Auntie Nan snips the Michaelmas daisies
and passes them to me.

Uncle Graham focuses and snaps
Mary on the swing;

his new camera can capture moving objects.
Smile, he says.

At first glance it's a day in which relatives are taking time out to nurture their children. There are flowers and a swing and a camera capturing a smile. Everything is as it should be in the world – children are precious and adults protect and value their innocence. But then there is:

Nan answers the door to a sad man
who asks for old clothes.

Without speaking, she gives him
Graham's working trousers.

Now there is a sad man and a solemn Nan who responds without question, without even speaking.

Unspoken grief runs through 'A Day Off' from the opening lines, we are never told what has happened but we know; hints are there in the mood and in the contrast of simple, joyful moments with the extraordinary image of:

At the school gate, mothers cry
and claw at the mud.

—

What happens in these poems is specific to this childhood in that valley, yet these adults and their unexpected reactions could belong to anyone living anywhere:

Forty-odd years since her old man caught her.
Dobbed in by Trebor Mints and cheap cologne.
But there was no reprimand, he just said,
'Be open but hands off my Woodbines.'

('A Mother's Love')

I couldn't have grown up farther away from Lynda's valley. I haven't met this family. Yet I know this place and I know these people. I would go so far to say that these kinds of experiences have happened to most readers. The conversation in 'A Mother's Love' could occur in any language on any continent.

The things which puzzle a child about the adult world will always be a thing to be examined, remembered and written about.

I rest my case. Lynda Nash is a poet and *Ashes of a Valleys Childhood* is a universally appealing, soulful first collection of poetry. Enjoy!

Barrie Llewelyn
University of Glamorgan, October 2009

Sunday's Child

Father chain-smoked, ears alert
for a signal of my arrival;
a bawl from inexperienced lungs
halted his pacing outside the wood-shed.

The cork popped early evening,
in the front bedroom
under Granny's supervision.

The old wives, anticipating my coming,
stood on door steps in Welsh aprons
gassing.

No carriage awaited the first-born
(*It's unlucky to buy before the birth*)

so trussed in woollen chains
I did the monkey parade
along High Street with Grandpa.
(*Your father might have dropped you.*)

Father took to bed
to hide his red face and bitter tears
cursing my disruption –
as if I had instigated this intrusion.

As if I had decided
on this first day of life
to cause derision.

Only Words

Grandpa taught me to read. He split infinitives
in the Daily Express with a blackened finger,
patiently sounding syllables until I understood.

While he worked underground, I played
librarian behind the armchair, rubber-stamping
adult literature for imaginary readers.

As his back broke, the hardbacks lessened
and the shelf bowed under the weight
of *Rupert's Adventures* and *Gulliver's Travels*.

One morning I caught my mother
about to put my school book on the fire.
She said, 'You know me, I'll burn anything.'

But I didn't.

Neither did I understand why
she sometimes lay red-eyed beside the hearth,
while Gran sat with a coat on,
coal dust under her nails.

Later, I stole a pile of books back from my cousin;
knickers bulging under a loose dress.
I wanted to pass those stories to my own children.

Few pages remain.

Grandpa taught me to read.
But only words.

Afternoon Shift

On his changing chair,
its white paint stained black,
he buttoned his stiff green shirt,
tightened his cracked belt another notch.

As he laced his steel-capped boots
he told me about his missing toe.
Removed in 1944. We were starving.
Your great-grandmother made soup.

The diversion misfired,
I cried anyway.

Easier to remove me from the kitchen,
take me for bread or to see the hydrangeas.
I'd be asleep by the time he came home,
his white skin stained black.

His Constant Companion

My friend Mike hated the bathroom
it reminded him of water and carbolic soap.
He enjoyed the fields –
could sniff out a hedgehog at twenty paces.
I took them home in a carrier bag,
Mother ranted about fleas.
We gave the creatures milky bread
but they were gone by morning.

Mike and I would jump the railway sleepers,
heading for the Bottle Field or the Cwm Farm.
But always, if I took my eyes off him,
he'd lope home, leaving me alone
in the unsullied greenery
spooked by sheep.

It's taken me over two hundred dog years
to realise that he did not like to leave the old man –
the one who taught him 'to sit' in Welsh.

Mike wasn't trained to fetch or beg,
but would walk the of length the valley and back
without leaving grandpa's side.

6pm to Midnight Man

Father was a Tuesday-Thursday-Saturday man
with *Brylcreem* and blue suit at six o'clock.
Ready to grace the flea-pits of the valleys
that doubled as dance halls.
Off to meet the boys
smelling of shaving soap and cigarettes.

Lacking cohesive words,
awestruck by his towering frame,
I wondered, instinctively, if he'd return.
Mother washed dishes
and sang along with Cilla Black
Anyone who had a heart...

Cut the sleeves off his shirts, said one neighbour.
Leave him! said another.
But Mam could only flounder.

And night after night,
shielded by banister rails,
we kids sat side by side, listening,
looking at each other,
saying nothing.

A Day Off

Auntie Nan snips the Michaelmas daisies
and passes them to me.

Uncle Graham focuses and snaps
Mary on the swing;

his new camera can capture moving objects.
Smile, he says.

I put the flowers in a vase; a sunny centre-piece
on the kitchen table.

Nan answers the door to a sad man
who asks for old clothes.

Without speaking, she gives him
Graham's working trousers.

On TV, men dig in rain. At the school gate, mothers cry
and claw at the mud.

Mam's Best Friends

Dad brought home many friends
from the pound when they came free.
One Alsatian, (*fabulously child-friendly*)
vaulted our back wall –
apparently the chicken wire was loose.

No time for melancholy,
a sheepdog pup with a teddy bear face
took its place.
A farmer needed him
(and we never did get to visit the farm.)

All varieties of canines came
for short sojourns at Dad's pleasure.
But he had little time for leisurely walks
being always busy wearing his suit
and playing the field.

We asked Mam why he left the dogs home.
She said, 'There's enough already where he's gone.'
and she wished some of *them* would disappear.

We asked how long before he picked up the next one?
but Mam just growled.

Picking Celandines

That day we were up on the mountain
in the gap
where the river runs.

He showed me the ruins
of a house.
He didn't know who lived there.

Now it was inhabited by cows.
Cows standing
knee deep in their own excrement.

I don't remember the smell
or the wind
or if we had wine gums.

I can still see his mouth
moving
but I don't recall what he said.

I know we went upwards after.
Probably
to another ruin; an older one,

where we'd sit a while
and look down
on the rest of the valley.

Ty Gwyn

1.

Evenings saw Gran
in her basket chair –
beside the sailor's chest
with a yellowing picture
of Queen Victoria
inside the lid –
knitting tea-cosies
for the chapel sale.

The narrow bathroom
off the kitchen
housed a white Belfast
cracked and etched
by three generations
of children making
rose petal perfume.

A Formica board
held pots and pans
over the bath
that became the toilet
on winter nights.

2.

Grandpa scrubbed
with hard green soap
that smelled like peas.

His top half looked
as if he wore a T-shirt
that shined white against
his coal-dust tattoos.

We played snap.
The Formica board
kept his modestly
and my innocence.

Roach End

'It's only a black-pat,' she said
as she broke its back with her thumbnail.
Dark blood spilled onto the carpet
where it couldn't be seen.

'It's gone now,' she said
as if there was only ever one of its kind.
I stopped screaming.

She picked up the squashed shell with her fingers
and threw it on the fire
where it hissed and crackled
and gave off a blue flame.
'Time for tea,' she said.

A Mother's Love

Forty-odd years since her old man caught her.
Dobbed in by Trebor Mints and cheap cologne
but there was no reprimand, he just said,
'Be open but hands off my Woodbines.'

Mam smoked Embassy (tipped) those early years.
Never once blew rings we could twirl on our fingers
or puffed smoke like a dragon as we proud knights
straddled her back shrieking with glee.

In the clean morning air she'd greet her darlings,
eyes ablaze, stale lips curling.
Limbs twitching, shoulders hunched.

Wide-eyed and petrified I snatched safety with my siblings.
We held our breath as sallow fingers fished frantically in ashtrays.

Calming   on   discovery   of   a   suitable   stub.

We, the passive ones, kept our mouths shut
and prayed she had a light.

Surplus to Requirements

6pm, whatever the season, she was sent
to lie sleepless under army blankets
limbs itching, unpicking the stitching on the hems.
Listening to other children laughing.

Sometimes she'd sneak her dolls in;
they all had names and games to play,
but her mother would hear her and yell.

So Mary practised holding her breath
until no light crept from the sides of the blackout curtain
and the street fell silent.

Whilst in restless slumber she would call
out – but no sound came.
Awake again, she clutched the bedclothes
until her knuckles turned white.

Being Small

...so Mary took to hiding
in the cupboard with the gas meter,
The Holy Slippers,
her father's best shirt
and the brass plaque that made her scream
when she was three.
Or four.
It's a boy and girl holding hands.
Nothing to be afraid of.

In the Window

Her feet on the sill,
she hugs her knees
and mouths words onto the glass.

They block her view of the children
in the gutter
playing Jackie-Five-Stones.

She smiles
and waves
but not at them.

She wonders if the latch
would look like a question mark,
if she could push it that far.

The scrape of metal
and she is a bird,
her feathers caught on the wind.

The Epitome of...

He wanted to pick blackberries
the fat juicy ones at the top of the briar.

He wanted to cram them in his mouth
and let the juice run down his chin.

Help me, Mam, he said.

He clambered into the hedgerow.
He would pick enough for a pie.
He would carry them in his vest.

Help me, Mam, he said.

Get back here, she said in her I'm-not-joking voice.
Who'd you think's going to clean them?

Me.

And cook them?

She had him there, he was six –
how would he light the gas?

He untangled himself from the bushes.
Resigned.
What's for tea, Mam – chips?

She clipped him around the ear.

He watched her slouch
toward the cliff edge.

He remembered what his father told him
the day he left:
laziness doesn't run in our family, son.
She walks.

Tin Bath

for Anita B. – thanks for the memory

Like a grey cloud threatening to burst
it hung on the garden wall,
a haven for spiders and snails
that could live undisturbed for weeks.

My brother liked to hammer
on its dusty back
and send a hollow din around the yard.

I tried to ignore its existence
but that sound got me running.
Didn't everyone have dirt between their toes?

The day arrived when, creature free
(*Never mind the silver trails*),
it was carried like a royal sedan
and placed on a bed
of threadbare towels and old macs.

Saucepans of water bubbled
and the geyser hissed in eagerness
to fill its gaping grey orifice
for the not-so-eager girl from the corner house
and me.

Given no choice, we sat in the water
and my brother was allowed to watch.

Couldn't be Pleasant, a Permanently Full Mouth

She scared us speechless when we first saw her
bare, Revlon-framed gums.

Becoming braver, we made oblique references
to *The Bride of Frankenstein* (the only horror film we'd seen)
and laughed as she garbled in retaliation
like a person born deaf.

For seven days she spat esses and effed tee-aitches
at her jeering offspring.

Then came the perfectly aligned symmetrical tombstones.
Blocks of marble she sharpened her words on
once she'd regained the power of tongue.

She scared us speechless.

Certain Things Were to be Expected on a Chapel Trip

Tomato sauce sandwiches,
      warm orange squash,
            sun cream and sand on our skin.

 Oil-covered swimsuits,
      sunburn and calamine,
           fish and chips when we got in.

Kids on the back seat,
      John Brown's Body
           turned into a riotous farce,

and mothers hiding
      from whiskery maids
           who might have heard us sing arse.

Lucky for Some

My thirteenth – no birthday would surpass it!
The whiff of hot sausage rolls,
salmon paste sarnies,
the obligatory jelly and blancmange.
Dad procured a crate of pop off the wagon.

1971. A dual celebration,
the army liberated Johnny.
Nervous collapse, they said.
He brought beer.

Jenny Leach was courting Winston.
She looked like Chrissy Evert with brains.
I *so* wanted to be her – she had the best boy.
Tommy Jones, a divorcee
on sixty a day, could not compete.

We played Petula Clark on eight-track
in Mam's best room
and ran riot in the street
while Uncle Graham tried to corner my best friend.

Neighbours complained I'd used the F word.
The others had – especially the boys.
I got tagged 'wild child'.
Mothers warned their children,
'Keep clear of Mary an' her mob.'
They missed all the fun.

Funeral Pyre

Haunted eyes in plastic sockets.
Crumpled faces pressed against the polythene.
'Keep them safe,' I said
as they were carried off to Grandma's.

I arrived in time to see them burn.

And there I stood transfixed and taunted
by the look of pleasure on her face
as the hands that once held mine stoked the flames
and one by one my bears and babies
gurned and grimaced in the heat of the fire.

As the gases from their molten bodies
ascended from the earth,
all that remained
were the ashes of a valleys childhood.

Nowhere to Run

I kept running-away clothes
in a cardboard box in the outside loo.
Sewed lop-sided knitted squares into blankets
to keep me warm on the street.

Mam kept the rent up the chimney
so it wouldn't burn through Father's fingers.
When I saw the back of his hand
my brother ran over the road –

they'd always run after him,
couldn't risk the neighbours knowing.
Keep up appearances. Don't let the side down.
Tell and you won't know what's hit you.

Once I dreamed of tiger's heads.
They spun around my bed.
I tried to jump out of the window.
Even in sleep there was no hiding place.

Hypochondria

If you heard his mother
beating seven years of schooling out of him
in the upstairs flat beside the cutting,
you would never doubt

why Price thought
every sniff pneumonia,
every spot cancer,
every headache a haemorrhage.

If you cut back at lunchtime
and heard Price sing
in tuneless agony
as he received his nourishment

or if on your way from school
you prayed your parents
would be out when you got home.
Then you'd understand.

A Good Morning

The bathroom door unlocked
I was not bathing or naked
but dressed in uniform
peering in the mirror.
His reflection startled me.

Did he say good morning?
I have no recollection.
Full of teenage insolence
I snapped inanities

without hesitation
or argument
no pause to ponder
the back of his hand
across my head.

I plastered blue eye shadow
on real thick after he'd gone.
At school no one commented.

Later one girl said she'd noticed.
I gave no explanation –
could it have made a difference?

My mirror turned inward;
a blurred unrecognisable reflection.
Mother always said,
'You'll meet the devil in that mirror.'
Perhaps I did.

Burning

Grandpa rocks on his heels
in the best room between divan
and coal fire, a pipe of *Golden
Virginia* in his dry mouth,
England's Glory in his hand.

He discards unlit matches
to the wicker basket beside
the hearth that contains yesterday's
news, which catches
my attention but not his.

He curses the sulphate;
it's not damp he's just too quick
tossing small sparks towards the paper
each strike threatening to push him
towards the bed or the grate.

The flames go unnoticed
contained within the newsprint
but I see them leap
and crawl along his trouser leg
as *Diawl!*

         he fights to keep his balance.

Pneumoconiosis

Pills as big as your thumbnail
placed in rows like a neat
production line of
panacea to mask the symptoms.
Prevention might have been
possible, but a cure was not.

Bedridden

a

words   florescent

dribbled   tube

from   lit

your   your

mouth   face

like a   so you

melting   couldn't

ice cube   see

you   what

couldn't   I was

swallow   saying

the
feather
pillow
became
a
head-
stone
the
vase
of
daffodils
a
tribute

Jubilee

1.

Red and white flags adorn the terrace railings.
Mothers spend hours making paper roses and carnations.
Children are allowed to wear Sunday best
and stay out past six o'clock.

The shops enter floats, and all the factories.
Workers wave and cheer in their garish costumes,
all eager to win a free hair-do
or fish and chip supper.

Stalls pepper the playing field; hoopla and coconut shy,
where floss-covered youngsters spend cadged pennies,
delighted to win cheap plastic toys
and eat hot dogs on the pavement.

The sun beams and the village sings,
hatchets are buried, feuds forgotten.
Time passes in a wealth of colour
and fathers swing babies in the air and laugh.

2.

Fathers load the factory lorries.
Shopkeepers chat about the weather.
Mothers scrub linoleum floors
and eke out the housekeeping.

Bins overflow with crumpled crepe.
Costumes adorn the ragman's cart.
The carnival is over.
But the children in the school yard still dance.

Retrospective

Newspapers emblazoned with lurid pictures
of bodies in basements
backstreet malingerers.
Beneath white dust sheets
smiley faces smirked
as flowers fell from hair to self-dug graves.

TVs screamed the moral outcry.
Bobbies brandished cuffs and fought
to drag death off pavements,
kicking and biting.

Hendrix was dead.
And mother in accusatory tone chided,
'Never accept sweets from strangers.'
She took aspirin for her head,
still knocked 'em back with Coca-Cola.

Life became a cryptic puzzle.
Cross words held hidden clues.
Alone at the door to adolescence
I endeavoured to fill in the blanks.

All the while prematurely-bereaved guitars wept.
I hid sherbet from my mother and wondered
'Jimmy who?'

Will Bach

I remember you – a shy lad,
stumbling on the path to manhood.
Your middle class friends
were bought with sweets and favours –
a leather belt is no teacher
of etiquette or social graces.

Father wasn't satisfied
until he'd cloned you as himself.
But a rogue gene surpassed his vanity,
grew aggressively out of proportion
(he paid the fines).

We should have discovered power in unity
but were separated by the very ones we sought to flee.
Coming together only to compare crimson silhouettes
of hands on white thighs.

You may have called for kinship
but I was searching for love and affection
inside my head
and didn't re-emerge for some fifteen years;
by then you were fighting your way back.

Shadowland

There is no warmth, no cold, just eerie stillness
in the light, which is neither day nor night but timeless.
I know it is 1am, though time has no motion.

They are both here – him and her –
but they are not my grandparents yet.
She carves bread, he sits at table,
the wireless plays swing.

Two ginger cats meander through chair legs.
I like the one with the round face,
the other is a shimmy shape.

Beyond the silence, the darkened passage –
I want to go home but I am scared.
Too scared to leave what death has left behind.
So I stay but do not sleep.

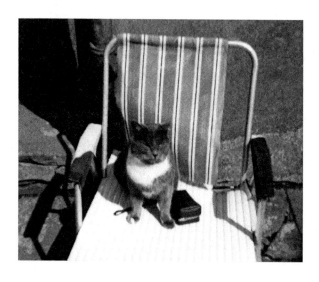

A Constant Reminder

Half way down the path she stops to comment,
on the disarray of jeans, tee-shirts and mismatched socks,
and re-informs me that red should never be hung next to white
as this means blood and bandages.

Mother was a war baby
but barely old enough to remember
the sentiment behind the red cross.

She raised her family on a balanced diet
of superstition and allegory
where holes got knocked in wood
and pounds of salt thrown over shoulders.

'It's unlucky to cry on your birthday,' she said.
But usually I did.
And I couldn't always remember what not to put on the table –
  shoes, umbrellas, the milk bottle?

Swords could be crossed – but not knives,
paving stones were hazardous,
and the consequences of washing on new years day
so terrifying I wouldn't go near a tap.

It became apparent that it was unclear
what she expected.
And I kept forgetting the rules.
If there are any rules in games of Catch-22.

Stack

It was dirty.
It stank.

The official notice served:
Housewives with Sunday-dinner mentalities
nod as they un-peg soot-specked washing.
Folk too frail for fracas – or too superannuated to care –
take cigarettes or cups of tea from their lips
to righteously sniff its final emission.

The blast is set:
Single figures say silent farewells.
As a lifetime collapses at their feet
it isn't tears of joy they weep.

The spark ignited:
A cloud covers the sun.
Men who'd placed their futures on open fires,
toss in their beds or prop up bars;
cursing political subverts with personal agendas.
Founding fathers turn in their graves.

It was dirty.
It stank.

Requiem

Hand in hand we step cautiously
across uneven ground where once stood
the pit-head baths, the locker room
and, in a fleeting memory from childhood,
I know we are getting near the reservoir
and should soon be able to see the remains of the canteen
where you ate sandwiches with hands that felt inside the earth,
smoked with lungs that breathed the dust of ages,
slurped black tea and laughed with Sid the Brace
about the bloke in the bucket shed
who couldn't tell left from right.
Much of your day was lost to darkness
where now all we see is rubble and light.

Black Gold

Small white hands collected it from the hillside
where the wind stung our ears
and the ground was fluid as we climbed.

A pseudo-mountain I told him.
Under the short coarse grass
is so much more
history.

He rolled it in his t-shirt,
carried it like a distended stomach.
I worried about stains,
finger marks on the furniture.

What shall I do with it now?

Put it on the fire
among the synthetic coke
and when the gas is lit
it may burn.

But he laid it on the hearth
like an offering.

Journey into Yesterday

A boat made of the past
would sail backwards
to this morning
through last night
and into the weeks gone by.

A boat made of the past
would sail out of the storm
and into the calm before
where the sun shines
and the wind is yet to blow.

A boat made of the past
would sail into the harbour
where you stepped on board
bought your ticket
and prepared for your trip.

A boat made of the past
would bob on the tide
cast its anchor in the sand
and wait for you.

About the author

Lynda was born and raised in the Rhymney Valley on the doorstep of the colliery and tar plant. After moving eighteen times in as many years she now lives in Trethomas with her husband, sons, and two cats. She teaches Creative English and Basic Skills in the community. Lynda's play *Ashes*, co-written with Daniel Curtis, is based on her poetry. Her short fiction and poems have been published in many magazines and her poem *Einstein's Theory* won The Aber Valley Arts and Literature Festival poetry competition 2007. Her first novel *Lily Strand* is a darkly humorous tale set in Cardiff.